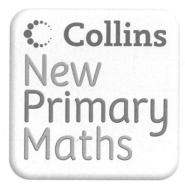

Collins
New Primary Maths

Pupil Book 4C

Series Editor: Peter Clarke

Authors: Jeanette Mumford, Sandra Roberts, Andrew Edmondson

Contents

All in order!

● **Order four-digit numbers**

① Write these numbers in order from smallest to largest.

a
| 4870 | 9350 | 2164 |

b
| 8142 | 4182 | 305 | 2841 |

c
| 2643 | 3462 | 4632 |

d
| 9406 | 4900 | 694 | 490 |

② Copy the following and write **<** or **>** between the numbers.

a 320 ☐ 190   b 670 ☐ 630   c 359 ☐ 272

d 271 ☐ 317   e 289 ☐ 298   f 523 ☐ 823

g 372 ☐ 284   h 477 ☐ 566   i 2190 ☐ 3990

① Write these numbers in order from smallest to largest.

a
| 6843 | 9682 | 6983 | 9863 |

b
| 3500 | 5300 | 3050 | 5033 |

c
| 2509 | 2905 | 5209 | 2059 |

d
| 7144 | 7523 | 7414 | 7325 |

② Put these weights in order, lightest to heaviest.

a 805 g   508 g   850 g   b 4613 g   4136 g   6413 g

c 995 g   599 g   1459 g   950 g   d 2244 g   4224 g   2424 g

③ Copy the following and write **<** or **>** between the numbers.

a 4294 ☐ 4492   b 9864 ☐ 9846   c 2496 ☐ 2469

d 4523 ☐ 2951   e 8516 ☐ 8592   f 3652 ☐ 3649

Explain how to round numbers to the nearest 10, 100 or 1000.

Decimals to one and two places

● **Use decimal notation for tenths and hundredths and partition decimals**

1 Copy and complete the following number lines.

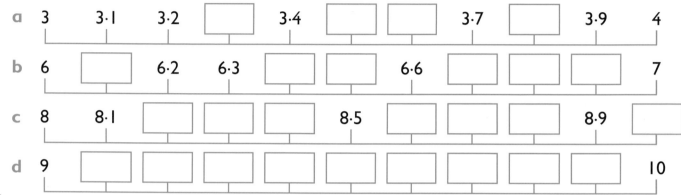

a 3   3·1   3·2   ☐   3·4   ☐   ☐   3·7   ☐   3·9   4

b 6   ☐   6·2   6·3   ☐   ☐   6·6   ☐   ☐   ☐   7

c 8   8·1   ☐   ☐   8·5   ☐   ☐   8·9   ☐

d 9   ☐   ☐   ☐   ☐   ☐   ☐   ☐   ☐   10

2 Write the decimal to one place that comes after these numbers.

a 4·2   b 5·1   c 6·8   d 3·5   e 2·4

f 9·7   g 1   h 8·3   i 4·9

1 Order each set of decimals from smallest to largest.

a   4·34   4·95   4·61   4   4·76   4·28   5
b   7·17   4·76   7·53   7·22   4·57   4·66   7·09
c   5·87   5·35   5·14   5·99   5·67   5·43   4
d   8·59   9·28   8·68   9·39   8·25   9   9·01

2 Look at the decimals from **1** c. Write them out again in order but this time write another decimal in between each pair of decimals.

3 Explain how you order decimals to two places.

1 What is the nearest whole number to these decimals?

a 8·83   b 6·24   c 7·17   d 8·98   e 23·56

2 Explain how you worked out the answers.

Adding and subtracting

● **Add or subtract pairs of two-digit numbers**

Write 5 addition and 5 subtraction calculations choosing two numbers each time.

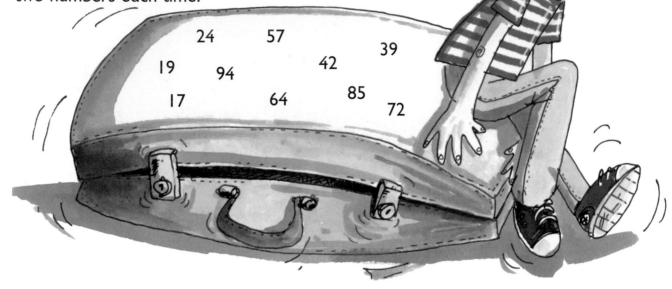

24   57
39
19   94   42
17   64   85
72

❶ Write 10 addition and 10 subtraction calculations choosing two numbers each time.

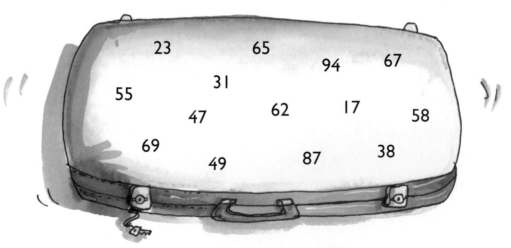

23   65
94   67
31
55
47   62   17   58
69
49   87   38

❷ Choose 5 of your calculations from question ❶ and check the answers by working them out in a different way.

The difference between a pair of numbers is 34. Find 5 possible pairs of numbers. Write an addition and subtraction calculation to go with each pair.

Racing addition and subtraction

● **Use written methods to add and subtract whole numbers**

$$
\begin{array}{r}
1\ 6\ 2 \\
+\ 3\ 5\ 4 \\
\hline
5\ 1\ 6 \\
\scriptstyle 1
\end{array}
\qquad
\begin{array}{r}
\scriptstyle 6\ \ 14 \\
7\ 4\ 6 \\
-\ 2\ 5\ 4 \\
\hline
4\ 9\ 2
\end{array}
$$

Write the calculations out vertically then work out the answers.

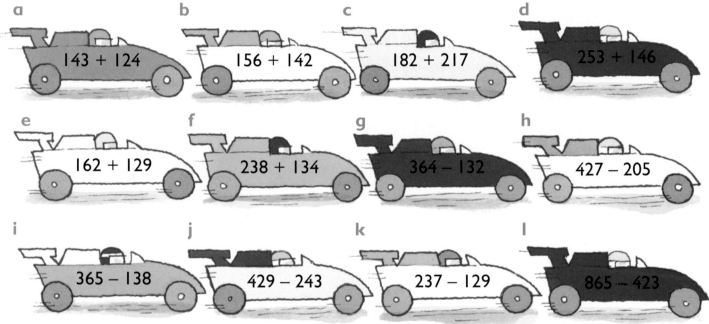

a 143 + 124
b 156 + 142
c 182 + 217
d 253 + 146

e 162 + 129
f 238 + 134
g 364 − 132
h 427 − 205

i 365 − 138
j 429 − 243
k 237 − 129
l 865 − 423

a 264 + 238
b 217 + 327
c 254 + 236

d 309 + 255
e 428 + 239
f 597 + 238

g 353 − 262
h 724 + 561
i 431 − 380

a 463 + 206 + 362
b 273 + 167 + 318
c 162 + 258 + 167

Negative numbers

Use positive and negative numbers in context

Draw an empty number line and write the numbers in the correct places.

a 0, −6, 8, −2, −4, 3, 1, 7

b −1, −7, 2, −5, 7, 4, 0, −2

c −10, 5, 9, −2, 3, −8, 0, 1

d −3, −9, 0, 2, 6, 10, −5, −1

Look at each thermometer and answer the questions.

a If the thermometer drops by 8° and then rises by 2°, what will the temperature be?

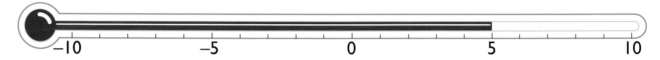

b If the thermometer drops by 4° then drops another 7°, what will the temperature be?

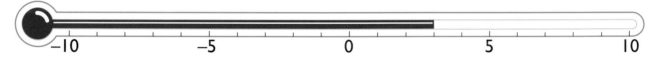

c If the thermometer rises by 7° then drops by 2°, what will the temperature be?

d If the thermometer rises by 11° then drops by 1°, what will the temperature be?

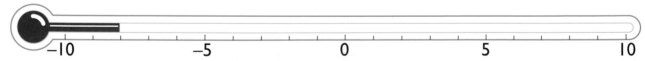

e If the thermometer drops by 8° then rises by 4°, what will the temperature be?

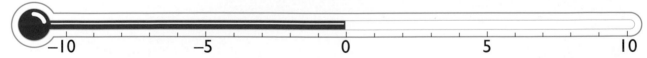

Work out these calculations. Use a calculator if you need to.

a −6 − 10 + 2

b 3 − 8 + 2

c 12 − 17 − 4

d 6 − 20 + 11

e 2 − 10 + 3

f 0 − 9 + 7

g 14 − 21 + 7

h −8 + 15 − 2

i 10 − 11 − 6

j −14 + 19 − 9

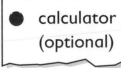

You need:
● calculator (optional)

Number sequences

Recognise and continue patterns

Copy and complete the number lines by filling in the missing numbers.

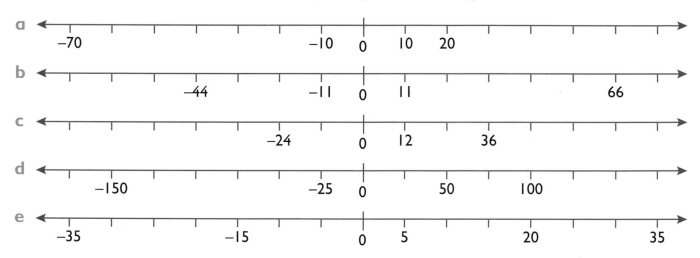

a −70   −10 0 10 20

b −44   −11 0 11   66

c −24 0 12 36

d −150   −25 0 50 100

e −35   −15 0 5 20 35

Look at the number sequences below.
Can you predict what numbers will come next?

1	2	3	4	5	6	7	8	9	10
11	12	13	14	15	16	17	18	19	20
21	22	23	24	25	26	27	28	29	30
31	32	33	34	35	36	37	38	39	40
41	42	43	44	45	46	47	48	49	50
51	52	53	54	55	56	57	58	59	60
61	62	63	64	65	66	67	68	69	70
71	72	73	74	75	76	77	78	79	80
81	82	83	84	85	86	87	88	89	90
91	92	93	94	95	96	97	98	99	100

1	2	3	4	5	6	7	8	9	10
11	12	13	14	15	16	17	18	19	20
21	22	23	24	25	26	27	28	29	30
31	32	33	34	35	36	37	38	39	40
41	42	43	44	45	46	47	48	49	50
51	52	53	54	55	56	57	58	59	60
61	62	63	64	65	66	67	68	69	70
71	72	73	74	75	76	77	78	79	80
81	82	83	84	85	86	87	88	89	90
91	92	93	94	95	96	97	98	99	100

You need:
- 1–100 number square
- 101–200 (or blank hundred) square

Use your own 100 square to copy and continue each pattern. Use a 101 to 200 square to keep the sequences going. What patterns do you notice?

Write the numbers that occur in each sequence in the correct order.

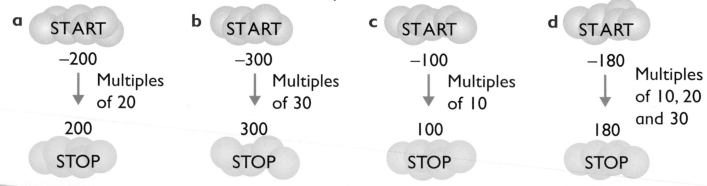

a START   −200 ↓ Multiples of 20   200 STOP

b START   −300 ↓ Multiples of 30   300 STOP

c START   −100 ↓ Multiples of 10   100 STOP

d START   −180 ↓ Multiples of 10, 20 and 30   180 STOP

Finding remainders

● **Find remainders after division**

Play 'Find the multiple'. Look at the numbers on the cubes below. Write the multiple that is closest to, but not greater than, each number in the shapes below them.

1 2	**2** 5	**3** 3	**4** 10	**5** 4
a 13	a 16	a 23	a 15	a 14
b 25	b 24	b 16	b 27	b 9
c 17	c 36	c 7	c 36	c 30
d 11	d 47	d 32	d 49	d 22
e 29	e 18	e 25	e 83	e 19
f 14	f 29	f 14	f 75	f 37

Look at each division calculation.
Write the multiplication fact you can think of to answer the calculation.
Write the answer to the calculation and any remainders.

1
a 36 ÷ 5
b 27 ÷ 4
c 52 ÷ 10
d 17 ÷ 3
e 25 ÷ 6

2
a 43 ÷ 4
b 23 ÷ 2
c 27 ÷ 8
d 39 ÷ 6
e 26 ÷ 3

3
a 35 ÷ 4
b 53 ÷ 5
c 29 ÷ 3
d 74 ÷ 10
e 15 ÷ 2

Example

43 ÷ 6
7 × 6 = 42
43 ÷ 6 = 7 R 1

Find the missing number to make each calculation correct.

32 = (6 × 5) + ☐
46 = (7 × 6) + ☐
56 = (5 × 10) + ☐
26 = (8 × 3) + ☐
19 = (4 × 4) + ☐

49 = (9 × 5) + ☐
436 = (4 × 100) + ☐
78 = (7 × 10) + ☐
367 = (3 × 100) + ☐
77 = (9 × 8) + ☐

Sports score division

● **Divide a two-digit number by a one-digit number**

Write an approximate answer to each division calculation.

a 26 ÷ 2   f 69 ÷ 3

b 69 ÷ 3   g 48 ÷ 4

c 88 ÷ 4   h 64 ÷ 2

d 46 ÷ 2   i 84 ÷ 2

e 55 ÷ 5   j 96 ÷ 3

Can I make
10 groups of …
20 groups of …
30 groups of …

Divide each score by the number at the beginning
of each row.

a
b
c

d
e
f

g
h
i

Use a written method to work out the answers to each
of the calculations in the ▢ activity.

11

Aeroplane division

Divide a two-digit number by a one-digit number

Approximate the answer to each calculation.

a 36 ÷ 3	f 64 ÷ 2	k 76 ÷ 4
b 48 ÷ 4 =	g 82 ÷ 2	l 57 ÷ 3
c 55 ÷ 5 =	h 93 ÷ 3	m 76 ÷ 2
d 84 ÷ 4	i 69 ÷ 3	n 84 ÷ 3
e 39 ÷ 3	j 46 ÷ 2	o 96 ÷ 4

Example

30 ÷ 3 = 10

Aeroplane seats are arranged in rows of 2, 3, 4 or 5.
Work out how many rows of each are full on these planes. Approximate your answer first. Record your working using a written method of division.

1
a 72 seats   b   56 seats
c 94 seats   d   38 seats

2
a 78 seats   b   48 seats
c 51 seats   d   87 seats

3
a 92 seats   b   76 seats
c 52 seats   d   68 seats

4
a 65 seats   b   90 seats
c 75 seats   d   85 seats

Use a written method to work out the answers to each of the calculations in the ▢ activity.

Rounding remainders

● **Round up or down after division, depending on the context**

Find the answer to these division calculations.
Be careful, some have remainders.

a 24 ÷ 4
33 ÷ 3
27 ÷ 5
18 ÷ 2
15 ÷ 4

b 29 ÷ 4
36 ÷ 6
23 ÷ 3
85 ÷ 10
90 ÷ 10

c 16 ÷ 4
22 ÷ 5
19 ÷ 3
34 ÷ 4
47 ÷ 5

Read each word problem. Write the division fact
and the answer. If there is a remainder, think
carefully whether you need to round your answer up or down.

a 27 people are going to the moon. Each rocket can take a maximum of 4 people. How many rockets are needed?

b There are 38 spacesuits. Each rocket has enough room for 5 spacesuits. How many rockets carry a total of 5 spacesuits?

c There are 34 helmets. Each astronaut needs 4 helmets. How many astronauts can travel into space?

d There are 52 weeks in a year. A rocket is launched every 10 weeks. How many launches in a year?

e 24 satellites are to be sent into space. 5 satellites can be sent a month. How many months until they are all up in space?

f Photographs of the rocket cost £6 each. I have £34. How many photographs can I buy?

Write 5 word problems for a friend to solve using space as the theme. Each word problem should include remainders that need rounding up or down. Try and make some of your problems two-step problems.

Use your facts

● **Use addition and subtraction facts**

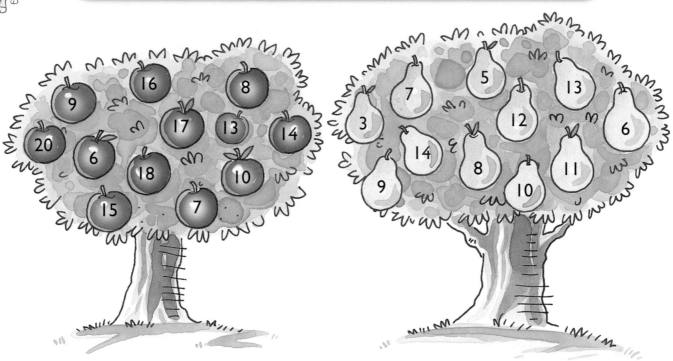

1 Choose one number from the apple tree and one from the pear tree to make 10 addition and 10 subtraction calculations.

2 Now write the multiple of 10 calculation that goes with each one.

Example
16 + 93 = 109

Example
160 + 930 = 1090

1 Choose one number from the apple tree and one from the pear tree to make 10 addition and 10 subtraction calculations.

2 Now write the multiple of 10 and 100 calculations that go with each one.

Example
17 + 95 = 112

Example
170 + 950 = 1120 and 1700 + 9500 = 11200

Use your knowledge of addition and subtraction facts to work out these calculations.

a ☐ + 30 = 140   **b** ☐ − 90 = 70   **c** 60 + ☐ = 190

d 500 + ☐ = 1200   **e** 1300 − ☐ = 200   **f** ☐ − 800 = 100

g 8000 + ☐ = 19 000 **h** 15 000 − ☐ = 4000 **i** ☐ − 7000 = 17 000

Money problems

● **Solve one-step and two-step problems**

Work out the answers to these word problems. Write down
the calculations you did to work out the answers.

a I wish I had £100, but I only have £37. How much more
do I need?

b My friend and I sorted 150 stickers into two piles.
70 were in one pile. How many were in the other?

c My plant has 67 flowers and my sister's has 42.
How many more flowers are on my plant?

d Our teacher told us to collect and bring in boxes. I
collected 34. My friend forgot to collect any so I gave him
18 of mine. How many did I take into school?

e The bike I wanted cost £200. Then the price went down
by £6. How much is it now?

a The shop ordered some new shirts to sell. 68 were
sold on the first day. 'If I can sell 87 shirts tomorrow I
will have sold them all,' said the shopkeeper. How many
shirts did he have to begin with?

b I earned £18 on Monday and £37 on Tuesday. Mum gave
me some money and now I have £58. How much did she
give me?

c The library van has 63 fiction books and 59 non-fiction
books. 89 books are lent to local schools. How many books
are left in the library van?

d At the school fair, Paula has a 'Guess how many sweets in
the jar' competition. I guessed 358 and my friend guessed
241. Paula said 'Put your guesses together, subtract 125 and
you'll know the answer.' How many sweets are in the jar?

Make up a two-step problem for a friend to solve.

Bookseller calculations

● Solve problems involving money, using a calculator

1 Use a calculator to work out the total price of the books in each box.

You need:
● calculator

a
£3.62
£2.27
?

b
£1.46
£2.31
?

c
£4.50
£3.37
?

d
£2.14
£3.43
?

e
£4.34
£1.35
?

2 Use a calculator to work out the price of the second book in each box.

a
£3.62
?
£8.24

b
?
£3.43
£9.17

c
£4.53
?
£8.51

c
£6.64
?
£13.27

d
£3.45
?
£7.99

e
?
£2.31
£14.68

You need:
● calculator

1 Use a calculator to work out the total price of the books in each box.

a
£4.53
£3.62
£3.62
?

b
£3.89
£3.07
£4.82
?

c
£4.35
£3.26
£3.12
?

2 Use a calculator to work out the price of the third book in each box.

a
£4.53
?
£5.24
£18.74

b
£7.64
£4.17
?
£28.36

c
£8.72
?
£4.82
£19.81

 Write a word problem involving money for a friend to solve.

Puzzles to solve

● **Report solutions to puzzles**

Solve the puzzles. Show all your working.

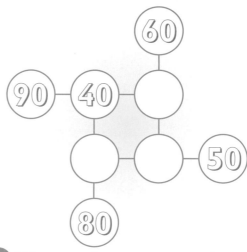

1 Write in the missing numbers.
Each side must add up to 100.

2 Write in the missing numbers so that each line of three numbers adds up to 150.

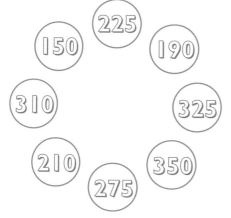

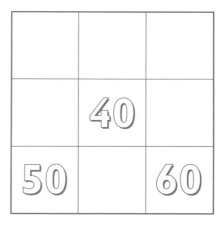

1 Find 3 pairs of numbers that make a total of 500.

2 Each side of this square and the diagonal must add up to 130.

3 Now choose one of the puzzles and explain in words how you solved it.

1 Write three tips for solving number puzzles.

2 Create a number puzzle of your own for a friend to solve.
Make sure you know the answer!

Number combinations

● **Solve problems and puzzles**

Each safe has a different combination of 3 numbers to open it.

The combinations all add to make a total of 15.

1 Find a combination for each safe.

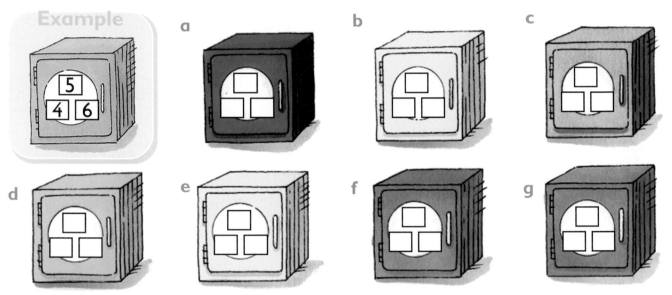

2 Explain how you worked them out.

 1 Arrange the numbers 1 to 9 in the circles so that the sum of the numbers along each side of the pentagon matches the number in the centre.

2 Explain what you have learnt about solving number puzzles.

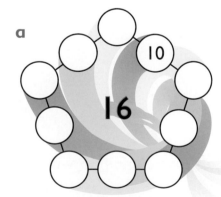

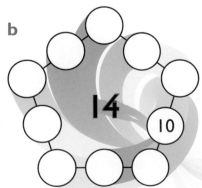

 Using the digits 1 to 9, complete the square so that all the rows, columns and diagonals total 15.

Finding multiples

● **Recognise multiples of numbers to 10, up to the tenth multiple**

Inside the treasure chest, lots of numbers were found.
Sort them into multiples of 2, 3, 4, 5 and 10.

Example

Multiples of 2 → 8, 12 …
Multiples of 3 →
Multiples of 4 →
Multiples of 5 →
Multiples of 10 →

Copy the Venn Diagrams below.
Sort the numbers 1 to 40 to match the labels.

a
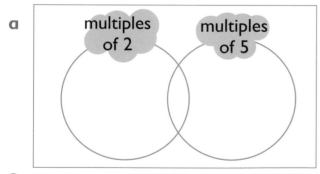
multiples of 2   multiples of 5

b
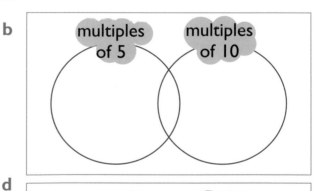
multiples of 5   multiples of 10

c
multiples of 3   multiples of 5

d
multiples of 3   multiples of 4

Draw your own Venn diagram.
Choose two multiples to sort,
and label the circles.
Sort the numbers 1 to 100.

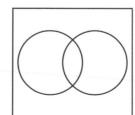

What if
you used
this Venn
diagram?

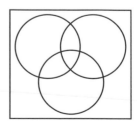

Mystery numbers

● **Solve mathematical problems or puzzles**

Find the mystery numbers.

a I am an odd number.
I am between 20 and 25.
I am a multiple of 3.
What number am I?

b I am a multiple of 10.
I am between 100 and 200.
My digits add to make a total of 3.
What number am I?

c I am less than 20.
I am a multiple of 3 and 4.
What number am I?

d I am a multiple of 5.
I am an even number.
I am between 81 and 99.
What number am I?

a I think of a number.
I multiply by 3 and then add 4.
The answer is 16.
What number am I?

b I am an odd number.
I am a multiple of 3 and 5.
I am less than 30.
What number am I?

c I think of a number.
My double is half of 100.
What number am I?

d There are two of us.
We have 2 in the tens place.
We are not multiples of any numbers except 1 and ourselves.
What numbers are we?

e I think of a number. I add 3
and then multiply by 3.
The answer is 33.
What number am I?

f We are between 10 and 100.
Our digits are the same.
We are multiples of 11.
What are we?

Write 3 mystery number puzzles for a friend to solve.

Missing numbers

● **Solve mathematical problems or puzzles**

Use the numbers 1 to 10 to make these statements correct. For each number sentence a different shape indicates a different number.

a

$$\triangle \times \square = 20$$

$$\bigcirc + \bigcirc = 14$$

$$\bigcirc \div \square = 5$$

$$\square + \square + \square = 27$$

b

$$\square + \bigcirc = 15$$

$$\bigcirc \times \triangle = 18$$

$$\diamond + \diamond + \diamond = 21$$

$$\bigcirc - \square - \square = 2$$

Replace the circles with the digits ⟨1⟩ ⟨4⟩ ⟨5⟩ ⟨9⟩ to make each statement true.

1 **LOST AND FOUND**

a $\bigcirc\bigcirc - \bigcirc = 36$

b $\bigcirc\bigcirc + \bigcirc = 63$

c $\bigcirc\bigcirc + \bigcirc\bigcirc = 100$

d $\bigcirc\bigcirc \times \bigcirc = 70$

e $\bigcirc\bigcirc - \bigcirc\bigcirc = 54$

f $\bigcirc\bigcirc\bigcirc + \bigcirc = 460$

g $\bigcirc\bigcirc \times \bigcirc = 49$

2 **LOST AND FOUND**

a $\bigcirc\bigcirc \div \bigcirc = 5$

b $\bigcirc\bigcirc + \bigcirc\bigcirc = 136$

c $\bigcirc\bigcirc \times \bigcirc = 135$

d $\bigcirc\bigcirc - \bigcirc\bigcirc = 46$

e $\bigcirc\bigcirc + \bigcirc\bigcirc = 64$

f $\bigcirc\bigcirc \times \bigcirc = 245$

g $\bigcirc\bigcirc\bigcirc - \bigcirc = 486$

Write 3 missing number puzzles for a friend to solve.

Doubling and halving multiples of 100

● **Derive quickly doubles of multiples of 100 to 5000**

1 Double each of these numbers.

a 27
b 44
c 33
d 18
e 39

2 Halve each of these numbers.

a 84
b 68
c 74
d 26
e 32
f 58
g 42
h 18
i 96
j 50
k 70
l 90

1 Find the multiples of 100. Double them.

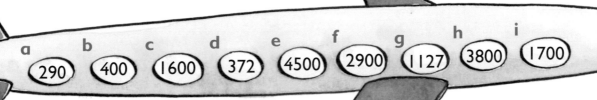

a 290
b 400
c 1600
d 372
e 4500
f 2900
g 1127
h 3800
i 1700

2 Find the multiples of 100. Halve them.

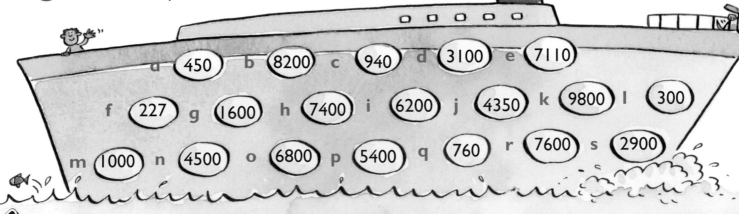

a 450
b 8200
c 940
d 3100
e 7110
f 227
g 1600
h 7400
i 6200
j 4350
k 9800
l 300
m 1000
n 4500
o 6800
p 5400
q 760
r 7600
s 2900

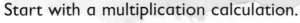

Start with a multiplication calculation.
Double each number to make a new calculation.
Keep doing this for as long as you can.
What do you notice about
each of your answers?
Does this always work?

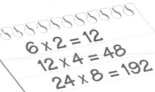

6 × 2 = 12
12 × 4 = 48
24 × 8 = 192

You need:

● calculator (optional)

Problems on safari

● **Solve one-step and two-step word problems**

The question for each of the word problems below is missing.
Read the problems carefully and write a question to match.

a Mr. and Mrs. Wallis hired a jeep for 1 week. The cost of the jeep for 1 day was £24.

b 4 groups of lions were seen altogether on safari. Each pride had 9 lions.

c The Wallises bought 2 pairs of binoculars for £54.

d Each day, for 2 weeks, Mr. and Mrs. Wallis took 10 photos of the animals

e 16 zebras, 2 lions, 12 hippos and 35 elephants were seen on Monday.

f The Wallises visited in the middle of summer. The hottest day had temperatures of 36°C. The coolest day recorded a temperature of 30°C.

Read each word problem.
Choose an appropriate method of calculating your answer.
● mental ● mental with jottings ● paper and pencil.

a Mr. and Mrs. Merton went on safari to Kenya. The total cost of travel insurance was £120 for 12 days. How much did it cost per day?

b The cost of hiring a jeep is £48 for 3 days or £98 for 7 days. Which deal costs less, per day? How much less?

c Over 3 days, Mr. and Mrs. Merton saw 27 rhinos. If they saw the same number each time, how many did they see each day?

d The hotel room cost £36 a day for the first 5 days and £27 for each day after that. How much does it cost to stay at the hotel for 8 days?

e The Mertons hired a local guide and a driver for 7 days. The guide cost £7 a day and the driver £9 a day. What was their total bill?

f Mr. Merton bought 2 large bottles of water for each day of the 12 day holiday. Bottles cost £3 each. How much did he spend on water?

Write 5 word problems for a friend to solve using safari as the theme.
Write one word problem involving each of the following:

● addition ● multiplication ● division
● subtraction ● more than one step

Folding and cutting

● **Make shapes by folding and cutting paper**

Fold your sheet of paper in half. Use 2 straight cuts from the fold line to make the shapes.

a 　　b 　　c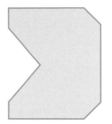

d 　　e 　　f

Example

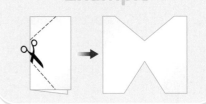

Fold your sheet in half, then in quarters.
Try to make these shapes using one straight cut only.

a 　　b 　　c

d 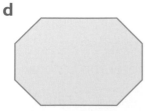　　e 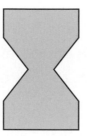　　f

Example

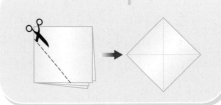

Fold your paper in half, then in thirds.
a With one straight cut,
   make three different symmetrical shapes.
b Mark the mirror lines and glue your shapes into
   your exercise book.

Example

cut here

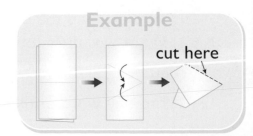

Shapes and symmetry

● **Draw polygons on squared paper that have more than one line of symmetry**

Make 4 L-shapes with interlocking square tiles.
Arrange the 4 L-shapes to make the shapes below.
Draw each shape on squared paper. Use colour to show how the L-shapes fit together.
Mark any lines of symmetry in black.

Example

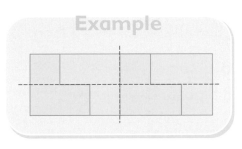

You need:
- ●●● 4 interlocking square tiles
- ●●● 1 cm squared paper
- ●●● coloured pencils
- ●●● ruler

a 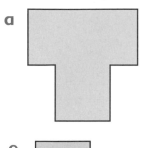   b    c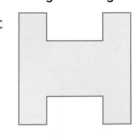

Work out how each shape is made using 4 L-shapes.
Record on squared paper and mark any lines of symmetry.

a   b   c   d

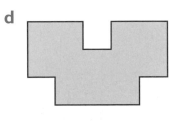

e   f   g   h

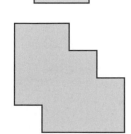   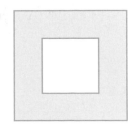

❶ Use your 4 L-shapes to make shapes with square holes. How many can you find? Record as before.

❷ Calculate the perimeter, in centimetres, of shapes **a** to **g** in question 2 of the ● activity.

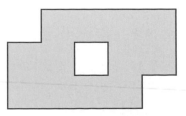

Nets of 3-D solids

● **Identify 3-D solids from their nets**

Use straws and Blu-tack to make these 3-D solids.
Name each solid you make.

a

Straws	Blu-tack
8 long	8 blobs
4 short	

Example

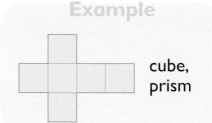

12 long
8 blobs   cube

You need:
● 8 long straws
● 4 short straws
● Blu-tack

b

Straws	Blu-tack
6 long	4 blobs

c

Straws	Blu-tack
6 long	6 blobs
3 short	

d

Straws	Blu-tack
8 long	5 blobs

1 Name the solid made from each net.

2 Which solids are prisms and which are pyramids?

Example

cube, prism

a
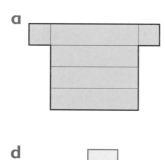

b
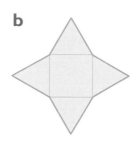

c
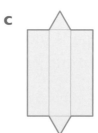

d

e
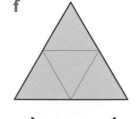

f
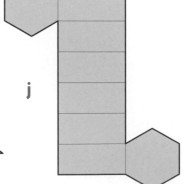

g
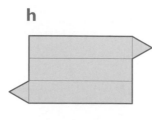

h
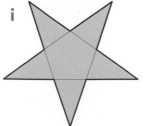

i

j

 For each pyramid in the activity, write the shape of its base.

Investigating 3-D solids

● **Make a model and draw a table to solve a problem**

Work with a partner.

1 Use all your cubes and build a cuboid.

2 Write a description of your cuboid.

3 Now swap papers.

4 Build each other's cuboids as described.

5 Have three more turns each.

You need:

● 24 interlocking cubes

● 3 pieces of paper each

Example

The cuboid is 3 cubes long, 2 cubes wide and has 4 layers

Work with a partner.

1 You can arrange 36 cubes to make a 6 × 3 × 2 cuboid.

How many different cuboids can you make with 36 cubes?

2 Make a table of your results.

Try to work in a systematic way.
Begin with 1 layer.

You need:

● 36 interlocking cubes

What if we had 48 cubes? How many different cuboids could we make? Perhaps 10?

10 at least. I predict 16.

1 Are either of the predictions correct? Investigate.

2 How many different cuboids could you make with 60 cubes?

3 Make a table of your results for 24, 36, 48 and 60 cubes. Write about the patterns you spot in the table.

4 Use your table to predict how many different cuboids you could make using 12 or 72 cubes.

Cut and slide patterns

● **Make and describe patterns by translating a shape**

Step 1
square

Begin with a square.

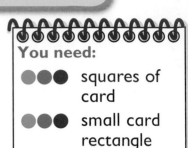
You need:
- ●●● squares of card
- ●●● small card rectangle
- ●●● plastic circles or semi-circles
- ●●● ruler
- ●●● scissors
- ●●● sticky tape
- ●●● A4 paper
- ●●● coloured pencils

Step 2
modify

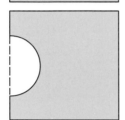

Make an alteration to one side and cut out a semi-circle.

Step 3
translate

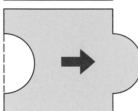

Slide the semi-circle to the opposite side of the square.

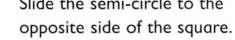
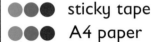

Step 4
new shape

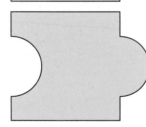

Make a repeating pattern with your new shape. Decorate two of your tiles.

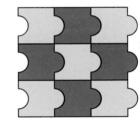

Take another square. Follow the steps to make this tile.
Decorate it in an interesting way. Make a repeating pattern with your new shape.

Step 1

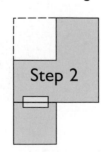
Step 2

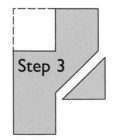
Step 3

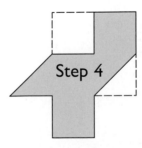
Step 4

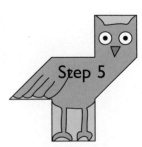
Step 5

1 Make 2 modifications and 2 translations to the rectangle of card to create a shape template.

2 Translate the template several times in all directions.

Fractions of a litre

● **Know the equivalent of $\frac{1}{2}$, $\frac{1}{4}$, $\frac{3}{4}$ and $\frac{1}{10}$ of 1 litre in ml**

Copy and complete.

a 1 litre = 500 ml + ⬚ ml

 = ⬚ ml

b $\frac{1}{2}$ litre = ⬚ ml + 250 ml

 = ⬚ ml

c $\frac{1}{10}$ litre = ⬚ ml

d $\frac{1}{4}$ litre = ⬚ ml

e $\frac{3}{4}$ litre = 500 ml + ⬚ ml

 = ⬚ ml

f $\frac{7}{10}$ litre = ⬚ ml

Write true or false for each of these statements.

a 500 ml = $\frac{1}{2}$ of a litre

b $\frac{1}{4}$ of a litre < 200 ml

c 700 ml < $\frac{3}{4}$ of a litre

d 100 ml = 1 litre

e $\frac{1}{10}$ of a litre = 100 ml

f 400 ml > $\frac{1}{2}$ litre

g $\frac{1}{4}$ l + 500 ml > 750 ml

h 800 ml < $\frac{3}{4}$ litre

1 a The carton of orange juice holds ⬚ ml

b It will fill ⬚ glasses.

c It will fill ⬚ beakers.

2 a The bottle of lemonade holds ⬚ ml

b It will fill ⬚ beakers.

c It will fill ⬚ glasses.

Millilitres more or less

● **Record readings from scales**

1 Write the amount of liquid in each measuring cylinder.

a	b	c	d	e
700 ml 600 ml 500 ml 400 ml 300 ml 200 ml 100 ml	700 ml 600 ml 500 ml 400 ml 300 ml 200 ml 100 ml	1000 ml 900 ml 800 ml 700 ml 600 ml 500 ml 400 ml 300 ml 200 ml 100 ml	1000 ml 900 ml 800 ml 700 ml 600 ml 500 ml 400 ml 300 ml 200 ml 100 ml	1000 ml 900 ml 800 ml 700 ml 600 ml 500 ml 400 ml 300 ml 200 ml 100 ml

Copy and complete the table for the cylinders above.

	Liquid in cylinder	Amount added	Total amount
a		300 ml	
b		150 ml	
c		430 ml	
d		190 ml	
e		580 ml	

1 Look at the soft drink containers.

How many millilitres altogether in:
a 1 can of lemonade and 1 bottle of orange?
b 1 carton of apple juice and 1 can of cola?

2 What is the difference in ml between:

a 1 can of lemonade and 1 carton of applejuice?
b 1 bottle of orange and 1 can of cola?

Fill up in litres

● **Write a capacity in millilitres to two decimal places**

These readings show the amount of fuel in millilitres
bought by each motorcyclist.
Write each amount in four different ways.

a 4500 ml

b 5500 ml

c 4250 ml

d 6750 ml

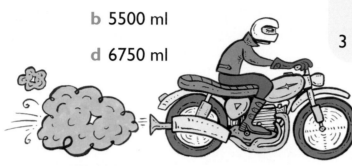

Copy and complete these petrol pump meter readings for motorcycle sales.

a 4100 ml = 4·1 l

b 6400 ml [____] l

c 7800 ml [____]

d [____] 9·2 l

e [____] ml 8·35 l

f [____] 12·64 l

These figures give the engine size in millilitres for each car.

a	b	c	d	e
1044	1395	1589	1616	2250

Copy and complete the table.

Car	Engine capacity in ml	Rounded to nearest	
		10 ml	100 ml
a	1044		
b			
c			
d			
e			

Chocolate bar sales

The table shows the chocolate bars sold by Mario's Shop in one day.

Chocolate bar	Number sold
Nutty choc	13
Chewy choc	5
Double choc	8
Chockee	18
Crunch choc	15

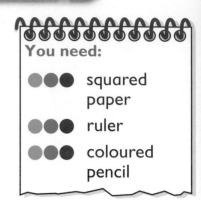

You need:
- ●●● squared paper
- ●●● ruler
- ●●● coloured pencil

Copy and complete the pictogram.

Chocolate bars sold by Mario in one day

Nutty choc							
Chewy choc							
Double choc							
Chockee							
Crunch choc							

Number of bars

○ stands for 5 bars

1 Copy and complete the bar chart for the data in the activity. Choose your own scale for the vertical axis.

2 Draw another bar chart. Use a different scale for the vertical axis.

3 Which bar chart displays the data more accurately? Explain your answer.

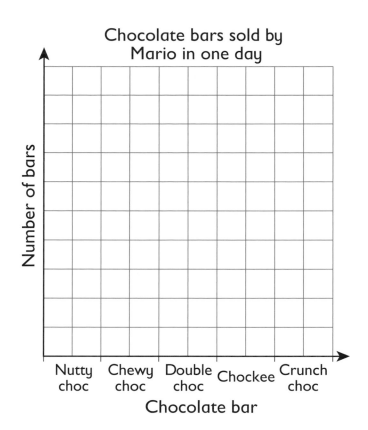

The table shows the supermarket sales of chocolate bars in one day.

Chocolate bar	Number sold
Nutty choc	55
Chewy choc	24
Double choc	45
Chockee	64
Crunch choc	40

1 Draw a pictogram for the data.

2 Draw a bar chart for the data.

3 Write three sentences that compare the sales of the supermarket to Mario's Shop.

4 Draw another bar chart for the data for the supermarket. Use a different scale for the vertical axis. Which chart displays the data more accurately? Explain your answer.

Game diagrams

1 Copy the Carroll diagram below.

	Red	Blue
less than 30	◯	◯
30 or more	◯	◯

● Write each number in the correct space on your diagram.

● Count the numbers in each space.
Write the totals in the circles.

a How many red numbers are 30 or more?
b How many blue numbers are less than 30?
c How many red numbers are there altogether?
d How many numbers are 30 or more?

2 Copy the Carroll diagram below.

	Odd	Even
Between 20 and 50	◯	◯
Not between 20 and 50	◯	◯

● Write each number in the correct space on your diagram.

● Count the numbers in each space.
Write the totals in the circles.

a How many odd numbers are there altogether?
b How many numbers are not between 20 and 50?
c How many even numbers are between 20 and 50?
d How many odd numbers are not between 20 and 50?

4   9   78   16   10   21   23   17   50   49   85   99   6   35   31   67   20   73   1   29   42   87   63   27   92   55

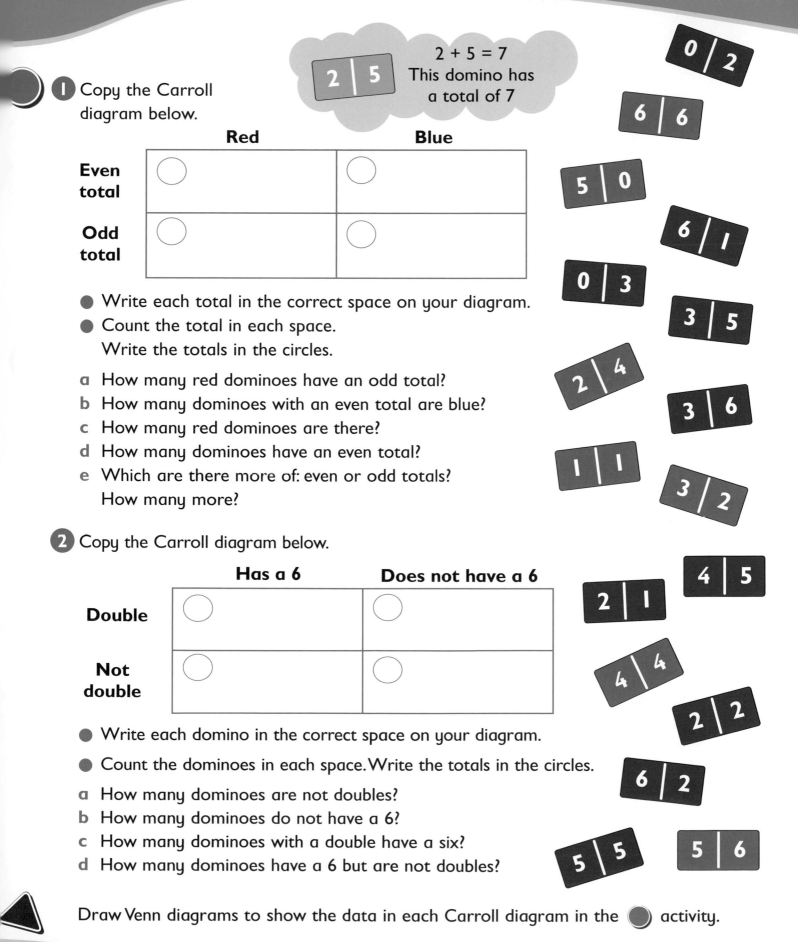

1 Copy the Carroll diagram below.

2 | 5
2 + 5 = 7
This domino has a total of 7

	Red	Blue
Even total	◯	◯
Odd total	◯	◯

● Write each total in the correct space on your diagram.
● Count the total in each space.
  Write the totals in the circles.

a How many red dominoes have an odd total?
b How many dominoes with an even total are blue?
c How many red dominoes are there?
d How many dominoes have an even total?
e Which are there more of: even or odd totals?
  How many more?

2 Copy the Carroll diagram below.

	Has a 6	Does not have a 6
Double	◯	◯
Not double	◯	◯

● Write each domino in the correct space on your diagram.

● Count the dominoes in each space. Write the totals in the circles.

a How many dominoes are not doubles?
b How many dominoes do not have a 6?
c How many dominoes with a double have a six?
d How many dominoes have a 6 but are not doubles?

Draw Venn diagrams to show the data in each Carroll diagram in the activity.

Traffic data

● **Think about an investigation, predict what might happen and decide how to go about finding information**

Jenny recorded the types of vehicle passing a school at around 3:30 p.m.

Vehicle	Number	Total
Bicycle	))))))))))))))))))))	
Car	)))))))))))))))))))))))))))))))))))))	
Bus	)))))))))))))	
Motorcycle	))))))))	
Lorry	))))))))))	

1 What is wrong with her tally chart?

2 Using the same data, draw and complete the tally chart correctly.

3 Which vehicle is the most common?

4 There were more cars than buses.

How many more?

5 In the next minute, 7 cars, 2 buses and 4 bicycles passed the school. Add this data to your tally chart. Circle the existing totals and write the new totals.

6 If the data were collected at 10 p.m., how might the data be different?

Some children collected this data from cars passing their school.

1 Copy and complete the two tally charts for the data.

Country car was made in	Tally	Total

Number of windows	Tally	Total

2 In which country were most cars made?

3 Which is the most common number of windows?

4 Make a tally chart for the numbers of letters in number plates.

5 Which is the most common number of letters?

6 How would the tally chart be different if it were made 50 years ago?

Country car was made in	Number of windows	Number of letters in number plate
Japan	6	4
UK	6	4
UK	5	5
Japan	7	5
USA	4	4
France	6	4
UK	5	4
Japan	7	5
Germany	7	5
Germany	6	3
UK	6	4
Japan	7	4
USA	4	5
USA	3	4
France	6	5
Germany	6	5
Japan	5	4
UK	7	4
Japan	7	5
Japan	5	3
UK	5	3
France	6	4
France	4	5
USA	6	5
Germany	3	2
Japan	4	4
Germany	6	4
UK	7	5
France	6	5
Japan	6	4

You need:
- squared paper
- ruler
- coloured pencils

Work in pairs.

Plan an investigation into the number of doors the cars which pass the school have.

1 Make a prediction.

2 Describe the data you need to collect and how you are going to collect it.

3 Carry out your investigation.

4 Decide the best way to display and present your data.

5 Write about what you found out.

Traffic charts

● **Present data in different ways**

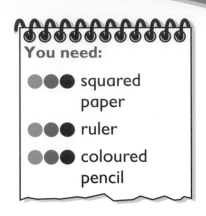

You need:
- ●●● squared paper
- ●●● ruler
- ●●● coloured pencil

The table shows the colours of cars passing a school.

1 Copy and complete the pictogram.

Car colour

 = 5 cars   Number of cars

Colour	Number
Silver	32
Black	17
White	13
Blue	9
Yellow	4
Red	27

2 Copy and complete the bar chart.

3 What is the most common car colour?

4 How many more red cars were there compared to blue cars?

Car colour

Number of cars (y-axis: 0, 5, 10, 15, 20, 25, 30, 35)

Colour (x-axis: Silver, Black, White, Blue, Yellow, Red)

5 Write 3 sentences describing the information presented in your pictogram and bar chart.

● Look at the table of information in the ● activity on page 37.

1 Draw a bar chart to show the number of windows.

2 Draw a pictogram to show the country in which the cars were made.

3 Copy and complete the Venn diagram.

4 Write 3 sentences describing the information presented in your pictogram and bar chart.

Cars passing school

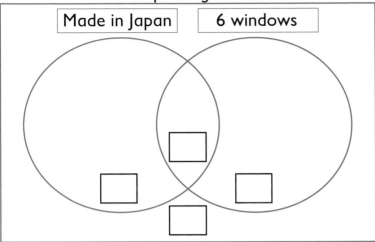

Made in Japan   6 windows

The table shows some information recorded from cars passing a school at 7 p.m.

1 Make a table to organise all the information.

2 Draw a bar chart to show the number of occupants.

3 Draw a pictogram to show cars with or without a hatchback.

4 Copy and complete the Venn diagram.

Cars passing school at 7 p.m.

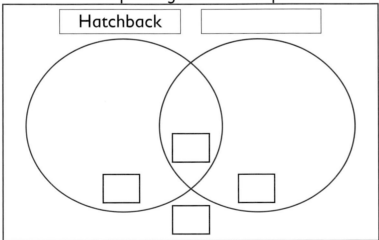

Hatchback

5 Write 3 sentences describing the information presented in your bar chart, pictogram and Venn diagram.

6 If the data were recorded when children were coming to school, how might it be different?

Number of occupants	Hatchback (Yes/No)
1	Y
1	Y
2	N
1	N
2	N
1	Y
3	Y
2	N
1	N
2	N
1	N
1	Y
4	Y
1	N
2	N
1	Y
3	N
1	Y
1	Y
5	Y
1	N
1	N
2	Y
1	N
1	Y
2	N
2	N
2	Y
1	N
3	N
1	N

Money box bar charts

1. Count the money saved by each child.

You need:
- squared paper
- ruler
- coloured pencil

2. Copy and complete the table.

Name	Amount saved
Jan	
Ajit	
Sam	
Vic	

3. Copy and complete the bar chart.

4. Use the information in the bar chart to answer these questions.

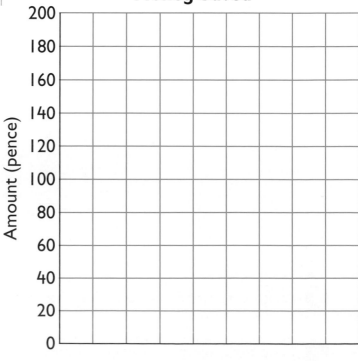

Money Saved

Amount (pence)

200
180
160
140
120
100
80
60
40
20
0

Name

40

5 a Which child saved the most?

b Who saved £1?

c Jan saved more than Ajit. How much more?

d What does the shortest bar show?

e How much money did Sam and Vic save together?

f Ajit's bar grew to the top of the bar chart. How much more did he save?

1 Draw a bar chart to show the savings.

2 Use the information in the bar chart to answer these questions.

3 a Which money box has the most money?

b What does the tallest bar of your chart show?

c How much money is there altogether?

d Which coins could be in the sweets money box?

4 Draw a pictogram to show the savings.

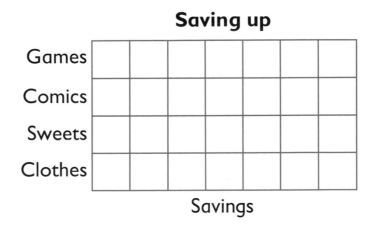

Saving up

Games

Comics

Sweets

Clothes

Savings

Key

Four children spent these amounts at the weekend. Sara: £2.80, Brian: £4.10, Seb: £1.30 and Dion: £3.90. Draw a bar chart and pictogram to show the data.

Energy savers

● **Present data using charts and diagrams**

An energy assessor inspected houses for loft insulation, wall insulation and double glazing. Mike, the assessor, made a table and pictogram to show the results.

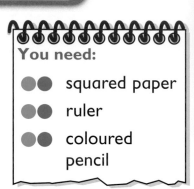
Energy saving	Houses
Loft insulation	13
Wall insulation	4
Double glazing	9

Energy saving in houses

1 What is wrong with Mike's pictogram?

2 Use the same data and draw the pictogram correctly.

Loft insulation

Wall insulation

Double glazing

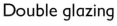

stands for 10 houses

Parker Electrical sells energy-saving devices.
The table and bar chart show their sales in June.

Electrical device	Number sold in June
Wind-up radio	24
Wind-up torch	9
Solar garden light	7
Energy-saving light bulb	32

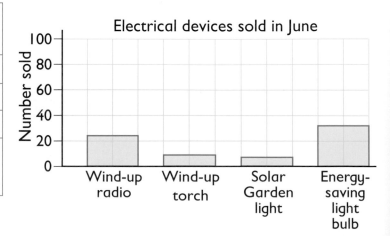

1 Why is the bar chart unclear?

2 Draw a bar chart that shows the sales more clearly.

This bar chart shows their sales in December.

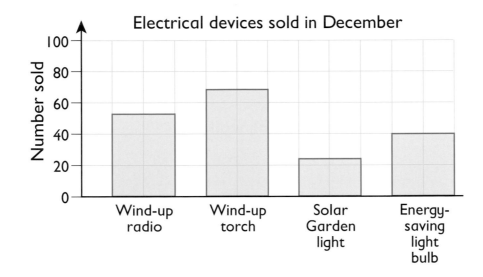

3 Write three sentences comparing the sales in June and December.

Householders were asked if they used energy-saving light bulbs. They were also asked if all their windows were double-glazed.

The Venn diagram shows the recorded information.

1 How many houses have both double glazing and energy-saving light bulbs?

2 How many houses do not use energy-saving electric light bulbs?

3 Copy and complete the Carroll diagram.

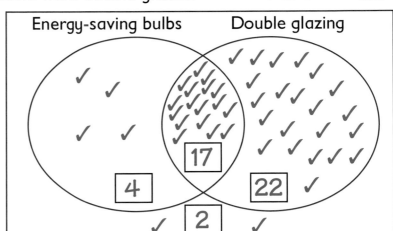

	Double glazing	No Double glazing
Energy saving light bulbs		
No energy saving light bulbs		

Travel diagrams

● **Use Venn and Carroll diagrams to present data**

Some children in Class 4 wrote down how they travel to school and how far.

1 Copy the Carroll diagram.

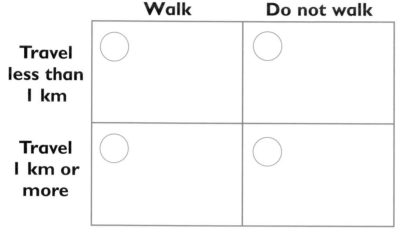

	Walk	Do not walk
Travel less than 1 km	○	○
Travel 1 km or more	○	○

2 Write the children's names to show how they travel to school.

3 Write the totals in the circles.

4 a How many children walk less than 1 km to school?
  b How many children do not walk to school?
  c How many children travel more than 1 km?
  d How many children wrote about how they travelled to school?

Jon	bus	$\frac{3}{4}$ km
Azul	car	4 km
Kay	walk	$\frac{1}{4}$ km
Siren	bike	$1\frac{1}{4}$ km
Rabi	walk	$1\frac{1}{2}$ km
Mark	car	10 km
Leon	walk	1 km
Sid	bike	$\frac{1}{2}$ km
George	bus	$2\frac{1}{4}$ km
Bao Bao	bus	$3\frac{1}{2}$ km
Aaron	walk	2 km
Poppy	walk	$\frac{1}{2}$ km
Colleen	car	2 km
June	bus	3 km
Hal	walk	$1\frac{1}{4}$ km
Allan	train	5 km
Fiona	walk	$\frac{3}{4}$ km
Sophie	walk	$\frac{1}{4}$ km
Gavin	car	$\frac{1}{2}$ km

1 Copy and complete the Venn diagram.

2 a How many children do not walk to school and travel more than 1 km?
  b How many children walk to school?
  c How many children walk less than 1 km to school?

Draw a Carroll diagram for the data using different headings.

How class 4 travel to school

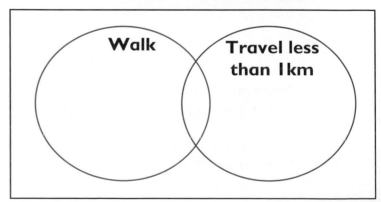

Walk   Travel less than 1km

Decimal amounts

● **Use decimal notation for tenths and hundredths**

Write the amounts using pounds and pence notation.

a   b   c   d

1 Write these prices in pence.

a £1.92   b £5.04   c £8.50   d £0.64   e £0.08

2 Write these prices in £.

a 461p   b 95p   c 230p   d 6p   e 403p

3 Write these prices in order, highest to lowest.

a £2.53 £3.52 £3.25 £2.35   b £0.90 99p £1.09 190p   c 92p £2.90 £0.29 209p

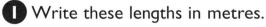

1 Write these lengths in metres.

  a 531 cm   **b** 208 cm   **c** 46 cm   **d** 9 cm   **e** 600 cm

2 Write these lengths in order, shortest to longest.

  a 2·47 m   0·47 m   4·72 m   2·74 m   7·24 m   0·27 m

  b 6·04 m   4·60 m   6·14 m   6·41 m   4·66 m   4·16 m

Shop calculations

● **Use written methods for addition**

Write these calculations vertically, then work the answers out.

a 243 + 318   f 264 + 352

b 436 + 125   g 383 + 121

c 349 + 203   h 475 + 252

d 237 + 214   i 286 + 281

e 346 + 138   j 198 + 421

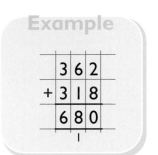
Example

Choose two items from the junk shop shelf and add up their cost.
Your teacher will tell you how many calculations to make.

a   b   c   d   e   f

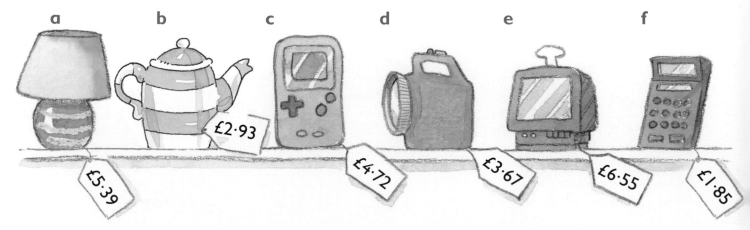

£2·93   £5·39   £4·72   £3·67   £6·55   £1·85

Choose 3 items from the junk shop shelf and add up their cost.
Your teacher will tell you how many calculations to make.

Boat calculations

● **Use written methods for subtraction**

Write these calculations
vertically, then work out
the answers.

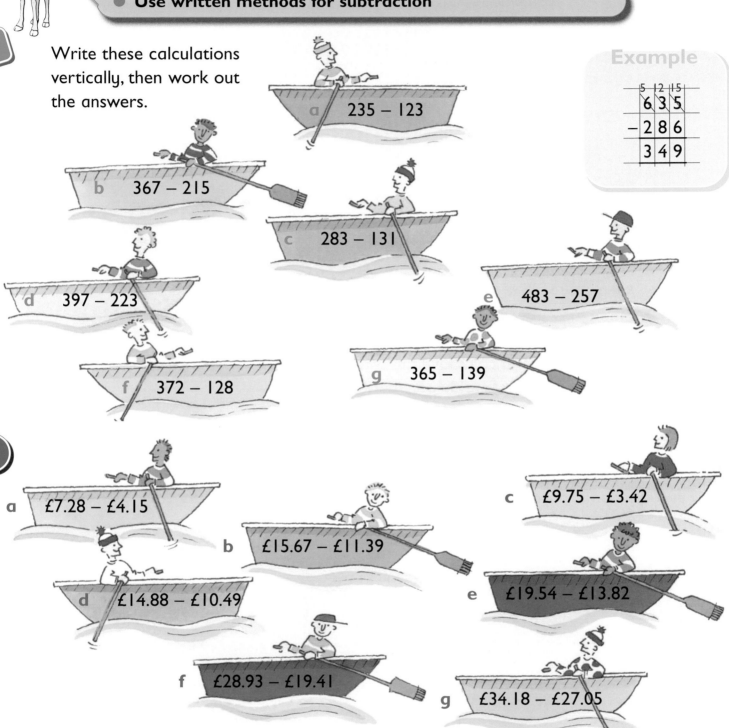

a 235 – 123

b 367 – 215

c 283 – 131

d 397 – 223

e 483 – 257

f 372 – 128

g 365 – 139

Example

```
  5 12 15
  6  3  5
– 2  8  6
  3  4  9
```

a £7.28 – £4.15

b £15.67 – £11.39

c £9.75 – £3.42

d £14.88 – £10.49

e £19.54 – £13.82

f £28.93 – £19.41

g £34.18 – £27.05

Use a written method to work out this word problem.
I have £16.84 in my hand. I want to buy a book and a pencil case that cost £8.37
and £3.64. How much will I have left?

Calculating capacities

● **Solve problems involving capacity**

I Each container is matched with a cup or a glass.

a  750 ml 150 ml

b  1 litre 200 ml

c 250 ml $1\frac{1}{2}$ l

d  1 l 250 ml 125 ml

Find the number of drinks you can pour from each container.
Use the cup or glass beside each container.

Use the bar chart to answer these questions.
 a Which container has the least capacity?
 b What is the capacity of the coffee pot?
 c How many cups of coffee can you pour?
 d How many cans of cola have the same
   capacity as the bottle of lemonade?
 e You pour 2 glasses of lemonade. How much
   lemonade is left in the bottle?

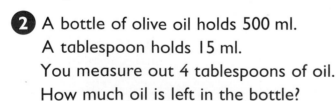

I When cooking rice, you need 3 cups of water
to every cup of rice.
You cook 4 cups of rice.
 a How many cups of water do you need?
 b A cup holds 200 ml. Which saucepan should
   you use: 2 litres, 3 litres or 10 litres? Why?

2 A bottle of olive oil holds 500 ml.
A tablespoon holds 15 ml.
You measure out 4 tablespoons of oil.
How much oil is left in the bottle?

3 In each 250 ml drink 50 ml is orange squash.
The rest is water.
How many litres of water do you need for 10 drinks?

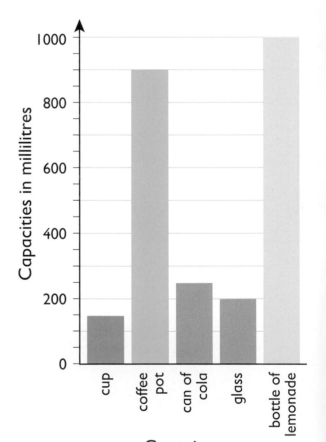

Capacities in millilitres

Containers

Postcard area

● Measure and calculate the area of shapes by counting squares

Choose a postcard. Cover the poscard with as many squares as you can. Write how many squares you need to cover the postcard. Now choose a different shape and repeat. Choose another shape and do the activity again.

You need:

● a postcard

● a supply of identical squares, rectangles, circles, coins and cubes

① Write the number of I cm cubes you need to cover the surface of each shape.

a   b   c   d

② Copy and complete.

a   Shape **a** is [ ] cubes smaller than shape **d**.

b   Shape [ ] is 2 cubes larger than shape [ ].

③ Count the number of green squares in each shape to find its area.

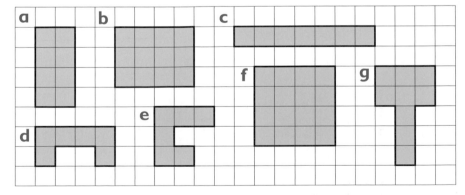

Place some small rods on the squared paper to design shapes, letters of the alphabet or names.

Count and colour the number of squares used to form each shape and record the area of each shape.

You need:

● coloured rods of lengths 2 cm to 5 cm

● I cm squared paper

Dotty shapes

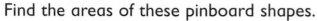

● **Find the area of rectangles and other shapes by counting squares**

Find the areas of these pinboard shapes.

a 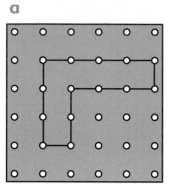   **b** 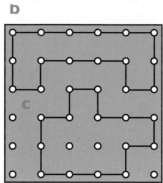 **c**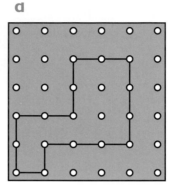

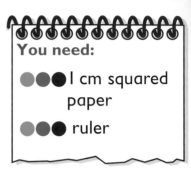

You need:

●●●I cm squared paper

●●● ruler

1 Draw these rectangles on I cm squared paper. Below each one write its area.

    a 6 cm by 3 cm   **b** 4 cm by 3 cm

    c 7 cm by 5 cm   **d** 10 cm by 2 cm

2 Draw these shapes on I cm squared paper.

    a $5\frac{1}{2}$ square centimetres   **b** $7\frac{1}{2}$ square centimetres

    c $9\frac{1}{2}$ square centimetres   **d** 16 square centimetres

Example

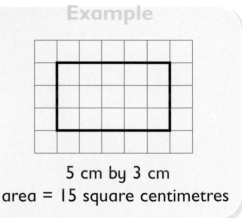

5 cm by 3 cm
area = 15 square centimetres

You can only see part of these rectangles and shapes. The area of each rectangle and shape is shown. Copy on to I cm squared paper and complete each one.

    a 12 square centimetres   **b** 14 square centimetres   **c** 21 square centimetres

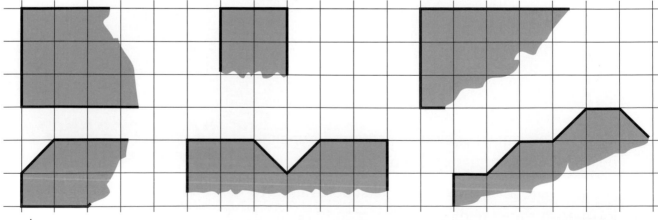

    d $8\frac{1}{2}$ square centimetres   **e** I I square centimetres   **f** 15 square centimetres

Shape puzzles

● **Find the area of shapes by counting squares**

a Make these shapes with interlocking squares.

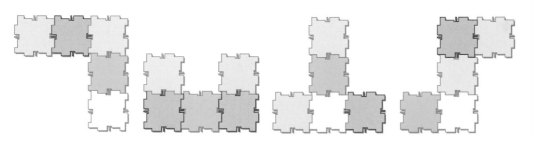

You need:
● 5 interlocking square tiles
● I cm squared paper
● ruler

b Draw each shape on squared paper and find its area and perimeter.

a Make these 3 pentominoes with interlocking squares.

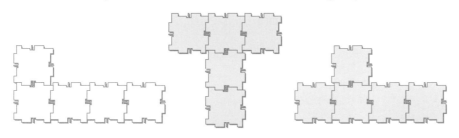

You need:
● 15 interlocking square tiles
● I cm squared paper
● coloured pencils
● ruler

b Make a 5 × 3 rectangle with your pentominoes. Draw your rectangle on 1 cm squared paper. Use colour to show how the pentominoes fit together.

c Write the area and perimeter of your rectangle.

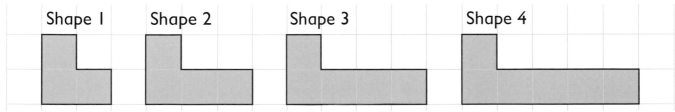

Shape 1   Shape 2   Shape 3   Shape 4

a Draw the next 2 shapes in the sequence on 1 cm squared paper.

b Copy and complete the table.

Number of shape	1	2	3	4	5	6
Area in cm^2						
Perimeter in cm						

You need:
● I cm squared grid paper

c Work out the area and perimeter of the 10th shape and explain how you did it.

Travelling times

● **Read timetables and use them to solve problems**

1 A bus leaves Market Street Bus Station in the town for these villages.
The bus takes 10 minutes between each village stop.
Copy and complete the bus timetable.

Market Street	10:15		
Winterby			12:45
Clarkham			
Langton		11:05	
Exford			

2 How long is the bus journey from Market Street to the village of Exford?

1 Flights leave Stansted Airport at regular intervals for Amsterdam.
The flying time between airports is 1 hour and 5 minutes.
Copy and complete the timetable.

Flight number	Depart Stansted	Arrive Amsterdam
1	6:40 am	
2	8:20 am	
3	11:25 am	
4	2:00 pm	
5	5:55 pm	
6	8:30 pm	

2 Flight number 2 takes off 35 minutes late. At what time does it arrive in Amsterdam?

3 You arrive in Amsterdam at 7:15 p.m. Which flight did you take?
How many minutes late did it arrive in Amsterdam?

4 Write two sentences about the information displayed in your completed timetable

Work with a partner.
Take turns to ask each other questions about the timetable. Try and make the questions as tricky as you can. But make sure you know the answers!

You need:
● local bus or train timetable

Fancy angles

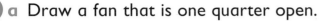

● **Estimate in degrees the size of an angle**

You need:

●●● 45°, 45°, 90°
   set square
   or half right
   angle
   measurer

●●● ruler

●●● coloured
   pencils

1 a Draw a fan that is one quarter open.
  b Divide it into 45° parts.
  c Colour the parts blue and yellow.

2 a Draw a fan that is half open.
  b Divide it into right angles.
  c Colour the parts green and red.

1 How many half right angles do these fans show?
Use a set square to help you.

a

b

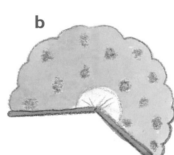

c

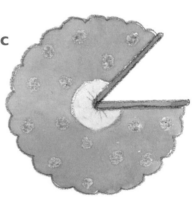

2 a Draw this fan shape.
   Colour 90° blue.
   Colour the 45° part yellow.

  b Find another way to colour the fan.

You need:

● 45°, 45°, 90°
  set square

● ruler

● coloured
  pencils

a Draw this fan shape.
   Colour 90° blue.
   Colour the 45° parts gold.

b Find three more ways to colour the fan.

c What if two parts are 90°. How many different
   ways can you colour the fan?

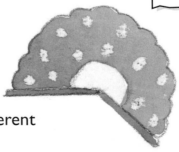

Getting in shape

- Know that angles are measured in degrees
- Solve mathematical shape problems or puzzles

Look at the shapes below.
Write the letters of the shapes which have:

a four angles of 90°

b one angle of 90°

c two angles of 45°.

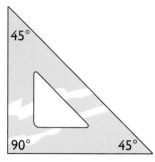

You need:

- 45°, 45°, 90° set square or half right angle measurer

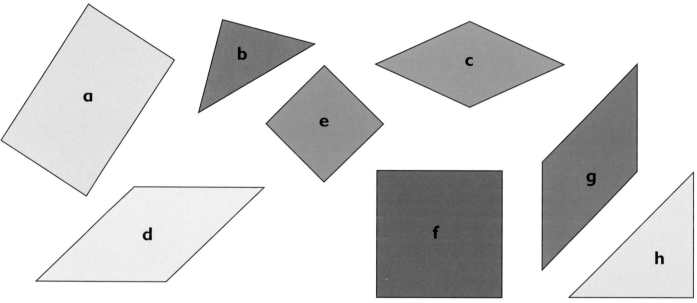

a Make this shape.

b *You can make 10 different shapes using 4 identical right-angled triangles.*

True or false? Investigate.
Draw each shape
you find.

You need:

- 4 identical right-angled isosceles triangles.

Remember

Shapes must be placed with
equal side against equal side.

Arrange the 12 straws to make 4 squares.
Make a careful
drawing of what
you did.

Remember

Bending straws
is not allowed

You need:

- 12 straws

Multiplying larger numbers

● **Multiply a two-digit number by a one-digit number**

Partition each of these calculations to find the answer.

a 45×4

b 15×5

c 24×3

d 18×4

f 37×4

g 43×4

h 36×2

e 26×5

i 41×5

j 29×3

k 27×3

1 Knock down the bowling pins using a ball of your choice. Multiply the number on the ball by the number on the bowling pin to get your score. Your teacher will tell you how many calculations to make.

26   43   63   16   37   62

24   45   35   37   54

14   29

3 5 6 4 9

2 What is the highest score you can make? Write the calculation.

3 What is the lowest score you can make? Write the calculation.

What if you used these bowling pins? Your teacher will tell you how many calculations to make.

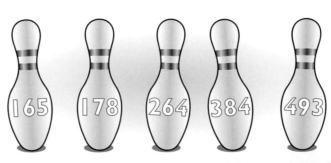

165   178   264   384   493

Multiplying larger numbers again!

● **Multiply a two-digit number by a one-digit number**

Use the colour code for each of the numbers to answer the calculations.
Be sure to estimate your answer first.

| 6 | 62 | 5 | 47 | 28 | 4 | 54 | 3 | 89 | 73 |

a ☐ × ☐ = ? b ☐ × ☐ = ? c ☐ × ☐ = ?

d ☐ × ☐ = ? e ☐ × ☐ = ? f ☐ × ☐ = ?

g ☐ × ☐ = ? h ☐ × ☐ = ? i ☐ × ☐ = ?

| 86 | 8 | 55 | 74 | 6 | 92 | 9 | 68 | 47 | 7 |

a ☐ × ☐ = ? b ☐ × ☐ = ? c ☐ × ☐ = ?

d ☐ × ☐ = ? e ☐ × ☐ = ? f ☐ × ☐ = ?

g ☐ × ☐ = ? h ☐ × ☐ = ? i ☐ × ☐ = ?

| 6 | 124 | 8 | 262 | 523 | 9 | 233 | 7 | 407 | 333 |

a ☐ × ☐ = ? b ☐ × ☐ = ? c ☐ × ☐ = ?

d ☐ × ☐ = ? e ☐ × ☐ = ? f ☐ × ☐ = ?

g ☐ × ☐ = ? h ☐ × ☐ = ? i ☐ × ☐ = ?

Dividing larger numbers

● Divide a two-digit number by a one-digit number

Approximate the answer to each of these calculations. Then use a written method to work out the answers.

a $84 \div 4 =$

b $84 \div 3 =$

c $93 \div 5 =$

d $77 \div 4 =$

e $72 \div 3 =$

f $71 \div 5 =$

g $84 \div 6 =$

h $93 \div 8 =$

❶ Hit the target using an arrow of your choice. Divide the number on the target by the number on the arrow to get your score. Your teacher will tell you how many calculations

❷ What is the highest score you can make? Write the calculation.

❸ What is the lowest score you can make? Write the calculation.

What if you used these targets? Your teacher will tell you how many calculations to make.

Dividing larger numbers again!

● **Divide a two-digit number by a one-digit number**

Use the colour code for each of the numbers to answer the calculations. Be sure to estimate your answer first.

5	95	4	84	62	3	77	6	58	43

a ▢ ÷ ▢ = ?   b ▢ ÷ ▢ = ?   c ▢ ÷ ▢ = ?

d ▢ ÷ ▢ = ?   e ▢ ÷ ▢ = ?   f ▢ ÷ ▢ = ?

g ▢ ÷ ▢ = ?   h ▢ ÷ ▢ = ?   i ▢ ÷ ▢ = ?

81	6	84	72	8	96	7	97	78	9

a ▢ ÷ ▢ = ?   b ▢ ÷ ▢ = ?   c ▢ ÷ ▢ = ?

d ▢ ÷ ▢ = ?   e ▢ ÷ ▢ = ?   f ▢ ÷ ▢ = ?

g ▢ ÷ ▢ = ?   h ▢ ÷ ▢ = ?   i ▢ ÷ ▢ = ?

0	1	2	3	4	5	6	7	8	9	÷	=	R

Investigate how many different division calculations with remainders you can make using the digit cards.

7	5	÷	6	=	1	2	R	3

5	6	÷	3	=	1	8	R	2

You need:

● set of 0–9 digit cards

● division symbol (÷) card

● equals symbol (=) card

● 'R' card

Raising money

Solve one-step and two-step word problems involving money

Read each word problem. Decide which operation to use. Approximate the answer then work out the answer.

a 4 children collected £5.37 each. How much altogether?

b Maria raised £37 for reading 4 books. How much did she raise per book?

c John's parents gave him a contribution of £3·30 each day of the school week. How much did he raise?

d A total of £98 was being sent to help 10 different children. How much will they each receive?

e Three countries will be given £57 each. How much altogether?

Read each word problem. Find the important information.
Write a calculation for each problem.
Give your answer in £.p where necessary.

a Joshua raised £23 for reading 5 books. How much did he raise per book?

b Year 4 had a skipathon to raise money. They made £61 for 2 hours of skipping. How much did they make each hour?

c Year 5 raised £64 from their sponsored silence. The silence lasted 10 minutes. How much did they raise each minute?

d Year 4 children raised £47 to send to 5 children in need. How much will each child receive?

e Tina saved up her pocket money for 4 weeks. She gave £13 to charity. How much pocket money does she get each week?

f £43 was raised in Year 3 over a 4-week period. How much did they raise each week?

Write 5 word problems for a friend to solve using raising money as the theme. Write one word problem involving each of the following:

● addition   ● subtraction   ● multiplication   ● division   ● more than one step

Freaky fraction machines

● Find fractions of numbers

Work out the numbers that come out of the machines. Show all your working.

Example

a

b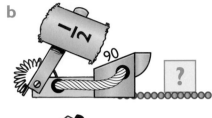

c

d

e

Work out the numbers that come out of the machines. Show all your working.

a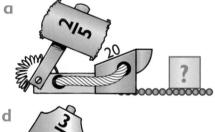

b

c

d

e

f

g

h

i

❶ Explain how to find fractions of amounts.

❷ How many different ways can you complete this statement?

 of 24 =

Ordering mixed numbers

● **Understand mixed numbers and position them on a number line**

1 What is a mixed number?

2 Write five mixed numbers in order starting with the smallest.

3 Put these mixed numbers in order starting with the smallest.

a $2\frac{1}{4}$ $3\frac{1}{4}$ $5\frac{1}{4}$ $3\frac{3}{4}$ $2\frac{3}{4}$

b $3\frac{1}{2}$ $4\frac{1}{2}$ $3\frac{1}{4}$ $4\frac{3}{4}$ $1\frac{1}{2}$

c $4\frac{1}{3}$ $3\frac{1}{3}$ $1\frac{1}{3}$ $3\frac{2}{3}$ $4\frac{2}{3}$

d $6\frac{1}{5}$ $6\frac{3}{5}$ $6\frac{4}{5}$ $6\frac{2}{5}$ 6

e $7\frac{3}{6}$ $7\frac{1}{6}$ $7\frac{5}{6}$ $7\frac{4}{6}$ $7\frac{2}{6}$

1 Draw a number line and put these mixed numbers in the correct place.

a $7\frac{1}{2}$ $8\frac{1}{4}$ $8\frac{3}{4}$ $8\frac{1}{2}$ $7\frac{3}{4}$ b $7\frac{3}{5}$ $7\frac{1}{5}$ $7\frac{4}{5}$ $7\frac{2}{5}$ $7\frac{6}{5}$

c $1\frac{2}{6}$ $2\frac{3}{6}$ $1\frac{5}{6}$ $2\frac{5}{6}$ $1\frac{4}{6}$ $2\frac{1}{6}$ d $5\frac{1}{8}$ $6\frac{3}{8}$ $5\frac{7}{8}$ $6\frac{4}{8}$ $5\frac{5}{8}$ $6\frac{6}{8}$

2 Choose six mixed numbers of your own to go on each of these number lines.

a 10 ⌷ ⌷ ⌷ 11 ⌷ ⌷ ⌷ 12

b 1 ⌷ ⌷ 2 ⌷ ⌷ 3 ⌷ ⌷ 4

c 8 ⌷ ⌷ ⌷ 9 ⌷ ⌷ ⌷ 10

Write down four mixed numbers that could come between $2\frac{1}{4}$ and $2\frac{3}{4}$.

HINT

You will need to think
of fractions other
than quarters!

Equal fractions

● **Use diagrams to identify fractions that are the same**

1 Copy the number lines. Fill in the missing fractions.

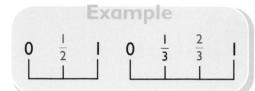

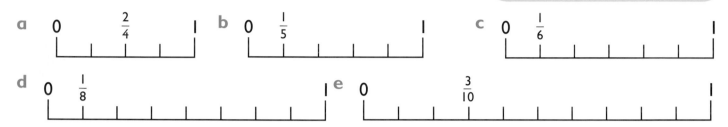

2 Look at the completed number lines from question **1**.

Circle all the fractions that are equal to $\frac{1}{2}$.

 1 Copy the table.

less than $\frac{1}{2}$	equal to $\frac{1}{2}$	greater than $\frac{1}{2}$
$\frac{1}{4}$	$\frac{2}{4}$	$\frac{3}{4}$

2 Choose one of the circles and copy it. Draw the circle as many times the parts it has. Colour its parts one by one. Write the fractions coloured in the table you drew from question **1**.

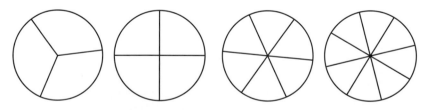

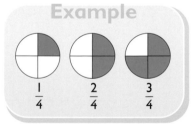

3 Choose other circles and repeat question **2** .

4 Look at the circles you have coloured. Can you identify any other equivalent fractions?

I coloured more than half a circle but less than $\frac{3}{4}$. What fraction could I have coloured?

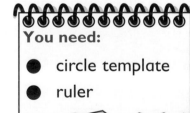

You need:
● circle template
● ruler

Fraction wall investigation

● **Use diagrams to identify fractions that are not the same**

1 What fractions can you divide each row on the fraction wall into to find fractions that are equal to one quarter?

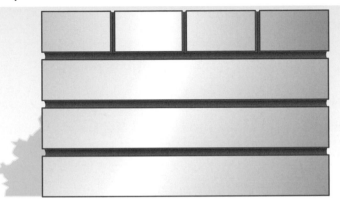

2 Now write all the equivalent fractions for $\frac{1}{4}$.

3 Now write all the equivalent fractions for $\frac{3}{4}$.

> **Remember**
>
> All the fractions must be divisible by 4.

1 What fractions can you divide each row on the fraction wall into to find fractions that are equal to one fifth?

2 Now write all the equivalent fractions for $\frac{1}{5}$ and then $\frac{3}{5}$.

3 What is the same about all the fractions on your fraction wall?

1 Investigate fractions that are equivalent to sixths.

2 Investigate fractions that are equal to sevenths.

Farmer fractions

● Represent a problem or puzzle using number sentences or diagrams

 1 Farmer Fred has four bags of hay. How can he share it equally between his three horses? Show your answer as a fraction. Draw a diagram to help you work it out.

2 Before he can give them the hay, he buys three more horses.
How much can each horse have now?

 1 Farmer Flo wants to share three bags of grain equally between her eight ducks. What fraction of the bags will each duck get? Draw a diagram to show your working.

2 The next day, she has five apples to chop up and share equally between her eight ducks. What fraction of the apples will each duck get?

 Make up a farmer fraction problem for a friend to solve. Remember, you must know the answer!

Daredevil decimals

● **Recognise the equivalence between decimals and fractions**

1 Copy and complete the number line.

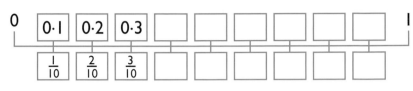

0 | 0·1 | 0·2 | 0·3 | | | | | | | 1

| $\frac{1}{10}$ | $\frac{2}{10}$ | $\frac{3}{10}$ | | | | | |

2 Write each mixed number or fraction as a decimal.

a 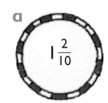 $1\frac{2}{10}$

b 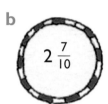 $2\frac{7}{10}$

c 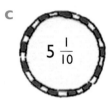 $5\frac{1}{10}$

d 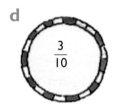 $\frac{3}{10}$

e 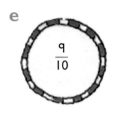 $\frac{9}{10}$

f 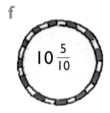 $10\frac{5}{10}$

3 Write each decimal as a mixed number or fraction.

a 3·4   b 0·8   c 12·2   d 0·6   e 35·3   f 0·1

1 Copy the number line.

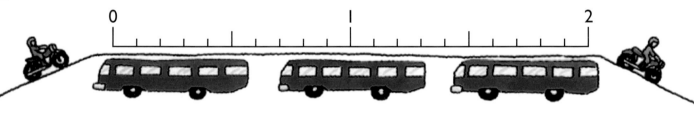

0   1   2

Write these decimals on your number line.

1·1   0·9   1·3   0·2   1·9   0·5

2 Write the equivalent fractions below the decimals.

3 Copy the number line.

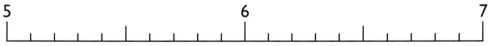

5   6   7

Write these fractions on your number line, then write the equivalent decimals below the fractions.

$6\frac{5}{10}$ $5\frac{1}{10}$ $6\frac{9}{10}$ $5\frac{5}{10}$ $6\frac{3}{10}$ $5\frac{7}{10}$

Design a diagram that shows the equivalences between decimals to one place and tenths.

Fractions and decimals

● Recognise decimals and fractions that are the same

1 Fill in the decimal number line from 0 to 1.

0   0·1   1

2 Fill in the fraction number line from 0 to 1.

0     $\frac{1}{10}$ 1

3 Both of the number lines above are in tenths; one is in fractions and one is in decimals. Use the number lines to find the equivalent decimal or fraction.

  a $\frac{1}{10}$ **b** $\frac{4}{10}$ **c** $\frac{7}{10}$ **d** $\frac{9}{10}$ **e** $\frac{3}{10}$

  f 0·6   **g** 0·8   **h** 0·5   **i** 0·2   **j** 0·4

1 Look at the number line. Choose one section to copy and complete.

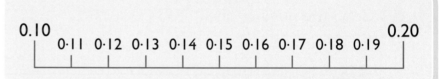

Example

0.10   0·11 0·12 0·13 0·14 0·15 0·16 0·17 0·18 0·19   0.20

0   0·10   0·20   0·30   0·40   0·50   0·60   0·70   0·80   0·90   1

2 Choose another section and repeat.

3 What are the decimal equivalents to these fractions?

  a $\frac{23}{1000}$ **b** $\frac{45}{100}$ **c** $\frac{67}{100}$

  d $\frac{12}{100}$ **e** $\frac{89}{100}$ **f** $\frac{56}{100}$

4 What are the fraction equivalents to these decimals?

  a 0·34   **b** 0·77   **c** 0·49

  d 0·04   **e** 0·95   **f** 0·18

Explain how you think you would order decimals to two places. Then write eight decimals to two places in order from smallest to largest.

Assorted biscuit problems

● **Use the vocabulary of ratio and proportion to describe the relationship between two amounts**

1 A biscuit has 3 cherries.

   a How many cherries on 2 biscuits?

   b If there are 9 cherries, how many biscuits are there?

2 Copy and complete the table.

Biscuits	1	2	3	4	5	6	10
Cherries							

1 Copy and complete the tables.

a

Buy 5 packets get 1 free gift

Packets	5	10	20			50
Free gifts	1			6	7	

b

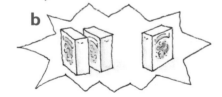

Packets bought	2		8		20	
Free packets		2		6		15

Buy 2 packets   Get 1 free

c

Buy 4 cakes get 1 free

Number of cakes	4		16			36
Free cakes		3		6	8	

2 How many biscuit men can you make using these shapes?

Look at questions 1 and 2 in the ● activity. Describe the relationship between the two different items using the words 'for every'.

Broken parts

● **Use the vocabulary of ratio and proportion to describe the relationship between two amounts**

1 Copy and complete the sentences.

a [1] out of [4] eggs are cracked.

b [ ] out of [ ] eggs are cracked.

c [ ] out of [ ] eggs are cracked.

d [ ] out of [ ] eggs are cracked.

2 Copy and continue each pattern.
Then copy and complete the sentences.

a 1 in every [ ] eggs are cracked.

b 1 in every [ ] eggs are cracked.

c 1 in every [ ] eggs are cracked.

d 2 in every [ ] eggs are cracked.

● Copy and complete the sentences.

a [ ] in 4 are broken.

[ ] in 8 are broken.

5 in [ ] are broken.

b 1 in [ ] are broken.

2 in [ ] are broken.

[ ] in 15 are broken.

c 1 in [5] plates are broken.

2 in [ ] plates are broken.

3 in [ ] plates are broken.

5 in [ ] plates are broken.

[ ] in 50 plates are broken.

d 1 in [ ] plates are broken.

2 in [12] plates are broken.

[ ] in 18 plates are broken.

6 in [ ] plates are broken.

[ ] in 60 plates are broken.

▶ Draw a picture to illustrate '2 in every 7'.

Counter fractions

● **Use the vocabulary of ratio and proportion**

Describe the number of blue counters in two ways.

Example

1 out of 2 are blue. $\frac{1}{2}$ are blue.

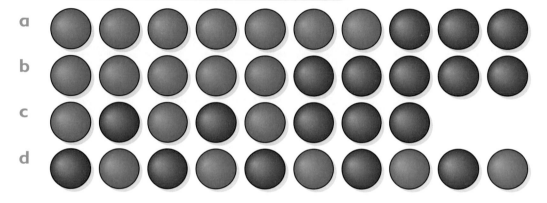

a

b

c

d

Work with a partner.

1 One person takes 10 counters from a bag.
The other person describes the blue counters.
Do this twice each.

You need:

● a bag

● red and blue
  counters

Example

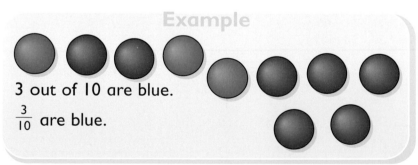

3 out of 10 are blue.

$\frac{3}{10}$ are blue.

2 Take turns to take 4 counters from the bag.
Describe the blue counters. Do this twice each.

If 3 out of every 7 counters are blue, how many blue
counters are there if the bag has 84 counters altogether?

Maths Facts

Problem solving

The seven steps to problem solving

1 Read the problem carefully. **2** What do you have to find?

3 What facts are given? **4** Which of the facts do you need?

5 Make a plan. **6** Carry out your plan to obtain your answer. **7** Check your answer.

Number

Positive and negative numbers

$$-10 \quad -9 \quad -8 \quad -7 \quad -6 \quad -5 \quad -4 \quad -3 \quad -2 \quad -1 \quad 0 \quad 1 \quad 2 \quad 3 \quad 4 \quad 5 \quad 6 \quad 7 \quad 8 \quad 9 \quad 10$$

Place value

1000	2000	3000	4000	5000	6000	7000	8000	9000
100	200	300	400	500	600	700	800	900
10	20	30	40	50	60	70	80	90
1	2	3	4	5	6	7	8	9
0·1	0·2	0·3	0·4	0·5	0·6	0·7	0·8	0·9
0·01	0·02	0·03	0·04	0·05	0·06	0·07	0·08	0·09

Number facts

Multiplication and division facts

	×1	×2	×3	×4	×5	×6	×7	×8	×9	×10
×1	1	2	3	4	5	6	7	8	9	10
×2	2	4	6	8	10	12	14	16	18	20
×3	3	6	9	12	15	18	21	24	27	30
×4	4	8	12	16	20	24	28	32	36	40
×5	5	10	15	20	25	30	35	40	45	50
×6	6	12	18	24	30	36	42	48	54	60
×7	7	14	21	28	35	42	49	56	63	70
×8	8	16	24	32	40	48	56	64	72	80
×9	9	18	27	36	45	54	63	72	81	90
×10	10	20	30	40	50	60	70	80	90	100

Fractions and decimals

$$\frac{1}{100} = 0·01 \qquad \frac{25}{100} = \frac{1}{4} = 0·25$$

$$\frac{2}{100} = \frac{1}{50} = 0·02 \qquad \frac{50}{100} = \frac{1}{2} = 0·5$$

$$\frac{5}{100} = \frac{1}{20} = 0·05 \qquad \frac{75}{100} = \frac{3}{4} = 0·75$$

$$\frac{10}{100} = \frac{1}{10} = 0·1 \qquad \frac{100}{100} = 1$$

$$\frac{20}{100} = \frac{1}{5} = 0·2$$

Calculations

Addition

Whole numbers
Example: 845 + 758

```
  845              845
+ 758            + 758
 1500             1603
   90              ₁₁
   13
 1603
   ₁
```

Decimals
Example: £26.48 + £53.75

```
 £26.48          £26.48
+£53.75         +£53.75
  70.00          £80.23
   9.00           ₁₁₁
   1.10
   0.13
 £80.23
   ₁
```

Calculations

Subtraction

Whole numbers
Example: 845 − 367

```
  845
− 367
   33  → 400
  445  → 845
  478
```

```
  700   130   15
  700   140    5
  800 + 40 + 5
− 300 + 60 + 7
  400 + 70 + 8
```

→

```
      7 13 15
      8 4 5
    − 367
      478
```

Decimals (Money)
Example: £39.35 − £14.46

```
  £39.35
− £14.46
   00.54 → 15
   24.35 → 39.35
  £24.89
```

or

```
       8 12 15
  £39.35
− £14.46
  £24.89
```

Multiplication
Example: 82 × 7

Grid method   or   Partitioning

```
×    80    2
7   560   14   = 574
```

```
    82
×    7
   560   (80 × 7)
    14   ( 2 × 7)
   574
```

→

```
    82
×    7
   560
    14
   574
```

→

```
    82
×    7
   574
    1
```

Division
Example: 87 ÷ 5

```
   87
 − 50   (10 × 5)      or
   37
 − 35   ( 7 × 5)
    2
Answer  17 R 2
```

```
5 ) 87
  − 50   (10 × 5)      or
    37
  − 35   ( 7 × 5)
     2
Answer  17 R 2
```

```
87 ÷ 5 = (50 + 37) ÷ 5
       = (50 ÷ 5) + (37 ÷ 5)
       = 10 + 7 R 2
       = 17 R 2
```

Shape and space

2–D shapes

    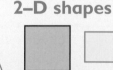

circle | right-angled triangle | equilateral triangle | isosceles triangle | square | rectangle | pentagon | hexagon | heptagon | octagon

3–D shapes

cube | cuboid | cone | cylinder | sphere | triangular prism | triangular-based pyramid (tetrahedron) | square-based pyramid